COUNTRIES OF THE WORLD

England

by Monika Davies

BELLWETHER MEDIA · MINNEAPOLIS, MN

Blastoff! Readers are carefully developed by literacy experts to build reading stamina and move students toward fluency by combining standards-based content with developmentally appropriate text.

Level 1 provides the most support through repetition of high-frequency words, light text, predictable sentence patterns, and strong visual support.

Level 2 offers early readers a bit more challenge through varied sentences, increased text load, and text-supportive special features.

Level 3 advances early-fluent readers toward fluency through increased text load, less reliance on photos, advancing concepts, longer sentences, and more complex special features.

★ **Blastoff! Universe**

Reading Level

Grade
K

Grades
1-3

Grade
4

This edition first published in 2023 by Bellwether Media, Inc.

No part of this publication may be reproduced in whole or in part without written permission of the publisher. For information regarding permission, write to Bellwether Media, Inc., Attention: Permissions Department, 6012 Blue Circle Drive, Minnetonka, MN 55343.

Library of Congress Cataloging-in-Publication Data

Names: Davies, Monika, author.
Title: England / by Monika Davies.
Description: Minneapolis, MN : Bellwether Media, Inc., 2023. | Series: Blastoff! Readers: countries of the world | Includes bibliographical references and index. | Audience: Ages 5-8 | Audience: Grades 2-3 | Summary: "Relevant images match informative text in this introduction to England. Intended for students in kindergarten through third grade"– Provided by publisher.
Identifiers: LCCN 2022018223 (print) | LCCN 2022018224 (ebook) | ISBN 9781644877173 (library binding) | ISBN 9781648347634 (ebook)
Subjects: LCSH: England–Juvenile literature.
Classification: LCC DA27.5 .D38 2023 (print) | LCC DA27.5 (ebook) | DDC 942–dc23/eng/20220420
LC record available at https://lccn.loc.gov/2022018223
LC ebook record available at https://lccn.loc.gov/2022018224

Editor: Elizabeth Neuenfeldt   Designer: Gabriel Hilger

Printed in the United States of America, North Mankato, MN.

Table of Contents

All About England

London

England is a country in Europe. It is part of the **United Kingdom**.

England's capital is London.
It is England's biggest city!

London,
England

N
W · E
S

England is mostly made of rolling hills. Low mountains rise in the northern **moors**. The River Thames flows in the southeastern **plains**.

Cliffs and beaches run along the country's coastline.

River Thames

Size: around 205 miles (330 kilometers) long

Famous For: England's longest river

England has warm summers.
Winters are mild.

The weather is very wet!
Rain falls all year long.
Fog is common, too.

fog

Many animals call England home.
Deer live across the country.
Skylarks fly overhead.

harbor seals

Animals of England

roe deer

skylark

harbor seal

European herring gull

Seals swim in the nearby seas. Herring gulls soar above the coastlines.

Life in England

England is home
to English people.
Most people speak English.
Many are **Christians**.

Most English people
live in cities. Some live
in the countryside.

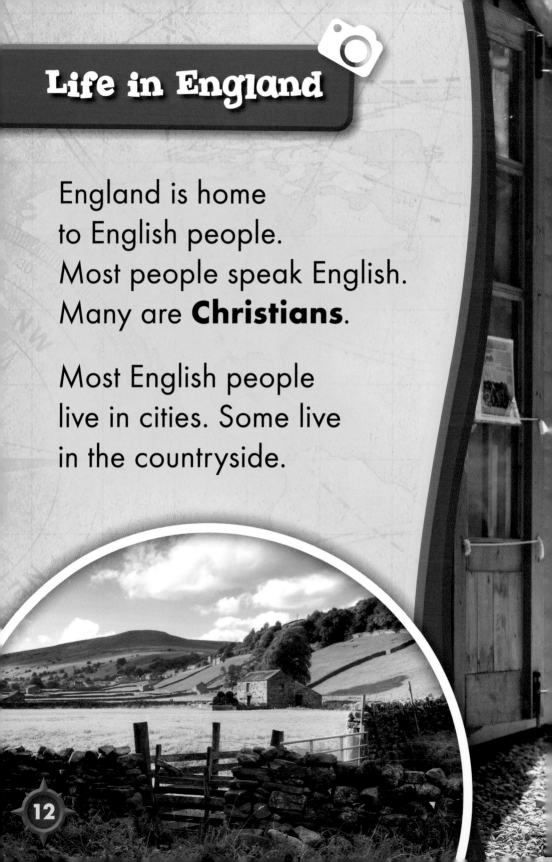

American English: Hello
British English: Hello

soccer

Soccer is England's
most popular sport.
Nearly everyone has
a favorite team!

People also love cricket and rugby. Some people hike and camp in the **Lake District**.

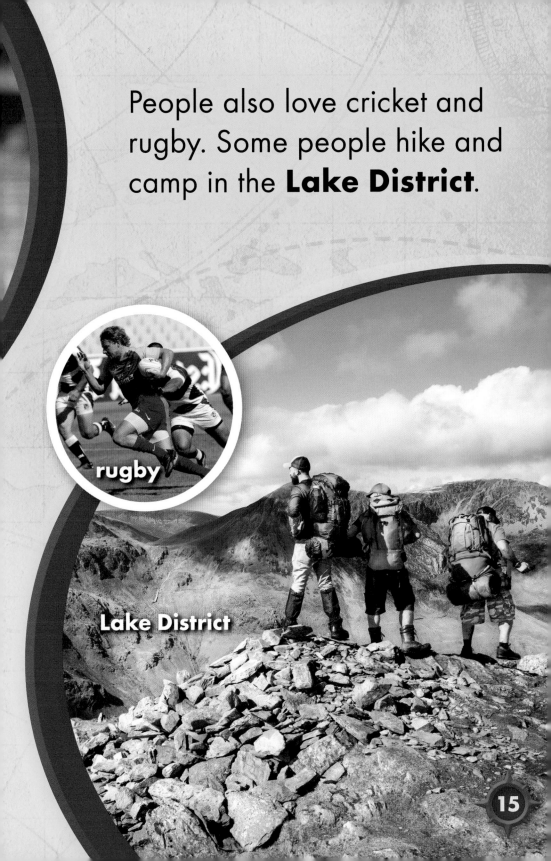

rugby

Lake District

Bangers and mash is a **traditional** English meal. It has sausage and potatoes. Fish and chips is another popular dish.

English Foods

bangers and mash

fish and chips

tea

biscuits

drinking tea

English people often drink tea with **biscuits** as a treat.

English people honor soldiers every November 11. It is called Remembrance Day.

Christmas

In December, Christians **celebrate** Christmas. People give gifts and eat. The next day is Boxing Day!

England Facts

Size:
50,301 square miles
(130,278 square kilometers)

Population:
57,148,150 (2022)

National Holiday:
St. George's Day (April 23)

Main Language:
English

Capital City:
London

Famous Face

Name: Emma Watson

Famous For: an actor and women's rights activist

Religions in the United Kingdom

Muslim: 4%

Christian: 60%

other: 10%

none: 26%

Top Landmarks

Big Ben

Stonehenge

Tower Bridge

Glossary

biscuits—cookies

celebrate—to do something special or fun for a big event, occasion, or holiday

Christians—people who believe in the words of Jesus Christ

Lake District—an area in northwestern England that has many lakes and peaks

moors—open, wet land that is not good for farming

plains—large areas of flat land

traditional—relating to the customs, ideas, or beliefs handed down from one generation to the next

United Kingdom—a country in Europe that includes England, Scotland, Wales, and Northern Ireland

To Learn More

AT THE LIBRARY

Dean, Jessica. *England*. Minneapolis, Minn.: Jump!, 2019.

Hansen, Grace. *England*. Minneapolis, Minn.: Abdo Kids, 2020.

Williams, Imogen Russell. *The Big Book of the UK: Facts, Folklore and Fascinations from Around the United Kingdom*. London, U.K.: Ladybird Books, 2019.

ON THE WEB

FACTSURFER

Factsurfer.com gives you a safe, fun way to find more information.

1. Go to www.factsurfer.com.

2. Enter "England" into the search box and click 🔍.

3. Select your book cover to see a list of related content.

Index